# Secrets of the Soul

# Secrets of the Soul

## Bohdi Sanders, PhD

**First Edition**

**Published by Kaizen Quest Publishing**

Printed in the United States of America

Library of Congress Cataloging-in-Publication Data
Sanders, Bohdi, 1962-
Secrets of the Soul

ISBN – 978-1-937884-05-5

1. Self-Help. 2. Personal Growth. 3. New Age/Spirituality. I. Title.

# Table of Contents

# About the Author

Bohdi Sanders is a lifelong student of wisdom literature, the healing arts, and the martial arts. His studies led him to explore the wisdom behind natural health, naturopathy, herbs, Reiki, Qigong, meditation and the power of the mind to heal the body, and to make positive changes in one's life. These explorations led to him earning doctorate degrees in naturopathy and in natural health.

Dr. Sanders is also a Certified Personal Fitness Trainer, a Certified Specialist in Martial Arts Conditioning, a Certified Reiki Master, and a Certified Master of G-Jo Acupressure. He holds a black belt in Shotokan Karate and has studied various other martial arts for over 30 years. He has worked with young people for over 20 years and is endorsed to teach in five different subject areas. He is the author of:

- *Warrior Wisdom: Ageless Wisdom for the Modern Warrior*
- *Warrior Wisdom: The Heart and Soul of Bushido*
- *The Warrior Lifestyle: Making Your Life Extraordinary*
- *The Secrets of Worldly Wisdom*
- *Secrets of the Soul*
- *Wisdom of the Elders*
- *Modern Bushido: Living a Life of Excellence*

Dr. Sanders' books have received high praise and have won several national awards, including:

- The Indie Excellence Book Awards: 1st Place Winner 2010
- USA Book News Best Books of 2010: 1st Place Winner 2010
- USA Martial Arts HOF: Literary Man of the Year 2011
- U. S. Martial Artist Association: Inspiration of the Year 2011
- U. S. Martial Arts Hall of Fame: Author of the Year 2011
- IIMAA Best Martial Arts Book Series of the Year 2011

**www.TheWisdomWarrior.com**

# Introduction

Self-knowledge is the
beginning of self-improvement.
*Spanish Proverb*

Do you really know what you believe and why you believe it? Are your beliefs and opinions formed by you during time spent in quiet reflection, or do your beliefs originate from the minds of others? Where do your beliefs come from? Do you ever take the time to just sit quietly and think about certain subjects and ideas, or is the only time that these thoughts cross your mind when you are listening to others debate the issues? These are all questions which must be addressed on your journey to self-awareness.

What are your beliefs? This is a simple question, but it is not that easy to answer. The term beliefs is defined as the acceptance by the mind that something is true or real, often underpinned by an emotional or spiritual sense of certainty. A belief is a statement, principle, or doctrine that a person accepts as true. This being said, everyone should know what his or her own beliefs are, after all, your beliefs are *your beliefs*, right? Well, yes and no. In today's society, we are bombarded from every side with media and other people trying to influence your thoughts with *their* beliefs.

You have to spend time in deep thought and meditation in order to ensure that what you believe is in fact, what *you* believe, and not someone else's beliefs which you have simply accepted as your own. Too many people just accept the opinions of the media and of those around them for their own beliefs instead of taking the time to ponder specific issues, philosophies, and ideas for themselves. You should never allow others to think for you; think for yourself. Socrates stated it concisely when he said, "The unexamined life is not worth living."

If you do not take the time to contemplate your own personal thoughts concerning specific subjects, how can you have any real conviction of the truth of your beliefs? Without considering the evidence, or lack of evidence, for yourself, how can you know that your beliefs are based on truth and rational thought, instead of myth or misinformation? In order to have a firm conviction in your beliefs, you have to spend time in quiet reflection, discerning the evidence and rationality behind your beliefs. You must know why you believe what you believe.

Our society has become one that craves constant media stimulation. The majority of people today are unsatisfied sitting quietly with their thoughts. Instead, they are constantly seeking to entertain their minds with some sort of outside stimuli, and there is always an abundance of outside stimuli eagerly waiting to occupy their minds. Television, movies, radios, computers, books, newspapers, friends, colleagues, and family, the list could go on and on, and all of these things compete for people's attention during their waking hours. Some people are even providing their minds with stimulation as they sleep, with stimuli such as subliminal CD's.

Although there is nothing inherently wrong with any of these things, they do seem to keep most people too busy to take time out for personal reflection. We all need time to be quiet, reflect, and meditate on who we truly are and what we really believe. Quiet time is essential to this process, and it is getting more and more difficult to slow down and find time for yourself in our fast paced society. It takes discipline and determination to resist the barrage of external influences which vie for your time.

The lack of time spent in quiet meditation and reflection has led to many people not really understanding who they are or what they really believe and why. If you were to ask someone what his or her philosophy of life is, there is a very good chance that you would not get a clear, concise, thought out answer. In fact, you would probably receive and answer similar to, "I don't know, I've never really thought about it." Most people simply haven't taken the time to think about it. This doesn't just apply to their philosophy of life, but it applies to most of their beliefs. Oh, they will often have strong opinions on different subjects, but when asked why they believe as they do, they will not have a rational reason, they "just do."

Developing a personal belief should involve forming an educated opinion which is based on evidence and rational thought, not on the politically correct rhetoric of the day. This is what makes you a unique individual. Your personal beliefs determine your individuality. Individuality distinguishes one person from another. If you do not take the time required to form your own opinions, you are not really acting as an individual, but rather just one of the mass of people who has allowed others to mold their thoughts to the agendas of others. By doing this, you have surrendered your individuality.

Developing your personal beliefs, your personal philosophy if you will, is vital in becoming a strong individual. Without developing your own personal beliefs, are you really living and thinking as an individual, or are you going through life mindlessly, your beliefs being influenced, if not controlled, by others? An awareness of your own individuality is called self-awareness. Developing your self-awareness is the goal of this book and will require you to develop your own beliefs, beliefs that come from time spent with your own thoughts.

Quiet contemplation is required to form specific beliefs that you know to be true, based on the evidence that you have personally examined and that you have thought about profoundly. Therefore, taking time for yourself is essential to understanding your beliefs, thus forming an awareness of your own individuality, leading to a true understanding of who you truly are and what you truly believe. This is true self-awareness, and helping you get to this point is the goal of this book.

*Secrets of the Soul* presents a series of questions that offer you the opportunity to develop a greater sense of self-awareness. It is not meant to be read quickly, but rather to be used as a guide. There are 101 thought-provoking questions which provide you with the foundation to start developing your core beliefs. Each of these questions is followed by a series of follow up queries to help you determine your true beliefs. Spend time pondering each question and form your own personal beliefs concerning the subjects which are presented.

Some of the questions will require more time and consideration than others, but every question will lead you closer to complete self-awareness and an overall understanding of who you are and what you really believe. More importantly, you will begin to understand why you believe what you believe.

You may find some of the questions intriguing, and others you may find embarrassing, but it is essential that you answer each question honestly. This is for your own self-awareness, and it will do you no good if you aren't honest with yourself during this process. If you aren't proud of some of the answers, you now have the opportunity to make some changes in your life, but remember to be honest.

The questions are grouped into specific categories, but it is not essential that you follow any certain order when contemplating your thoughts. You can meditate on the questions in any order that you see fit. You may also find that you enjoy discussing some of the questions with your family and friends, but I highly recommend that you develop your own personal beliefs before discussing a subject with others. This ensures that your beliefs are *your* beliefs, and not someone else's beliefs. Your goal is to develop a thorough understanding of your individuality, not someone else's. There is always a possibility of changing your beliefs after hearing someone else's point of view or discovering different facts, but it is important that you think for yourself.

I have also included quotes with each of the questions. These quotes are not meant to influence your beliefs, but rather to give you more to think about. Also, the quotes are not meant to reflect my beliefs, but are simply words of wisdom which I found interesting and applicable to the subject. I have not included my opinions or beliefs along with the questions; I merely expand each question to give you, the reader, additional things to think about while forming your beliefs. This is about your self-awareness, no one else's. In the end, it is up to you. What do *you* believe?

I hope you thoroughly enjoy your journey to self-awareness and truly discover what you believe and why you believe it. Here's to self-awareness!

# Bohdi Sanders, Ph.D.

We should know what our convictions are, and stand for them. Upon one's own philosophy, conscious or unconscious, depends one's ultimate interpretation of facts. Therefore it is wise to be as clear as possible about one's subjective principles. As the man is, so will be his ultimate truth.

Carl Jung

Get comfortable and search your soul for the real answers that reveal your hidden beliefs...

# Secrets of the Soul

Think for yourselves and let others
enjoy the right to do the same.
Voltaire

# Your Personal Philosophy

# Know Thyself!
## Inscription at the temple of Apollo at Delphi.

# 1

# What is Your Philosophy of Life?

Do you have a philosophy of life? If so, what is it? Is it based on truths or is it based on your biases and prejudices? Is your philosophy of life beneficial to you or does it seem to hold you back? Does it foster a good attitude towards others and life in general, or does it have negative connotations? Do you really feel good about your philosophy? If you don't have a philosophy of life, how should you go about developing one? What will you base it on? Do you really need your own or will you simply adopt someone else's?

Life consists in what a man is thinking of all day.
Ralph Waldo Emerson

# 2

# What is the Meaning of Life?

Are you on this planet for a reason? Is there a divine hand guiding you to your true purpose or are you going through life randomly choosing your direction as you please? What are you here for? Do you have a specific purpose to fulfill? If so, what happens if you die before you fulfill your purpose? Does your unfulfilled purpose get passed on to someone else or are you the only person in the Universe that can fulfill your purpose? What determines your purpose? God? You? Miscellaneous outside forces? How do you know?

Return to the root and you will find the meaning.
Sengsten

# 3

# Does Everything Happen for a Reason?

Is everything in life well ordered? Do you believe that everything happens as it should for a specific reason to help you on your life journey or do you believe that chaos rules the earth? Does a Higher Wisdom guide events in your life or is everything essentially random? Is there a plan for your life already mapped out or do you decide which direction your life will go? What do you believe? Why?

Everything in nature is a cause
from which there flows some effect.
Baruch Spinoza

# 4

# When Does Life Begin?

Does life begin at conception or at birth? What do you base your belief on? Is there any evidence to back up your belief? Is your opinion on this subject based on science, religion, or something else? What determines life? Is it breath? A beating heart? A single cell? Is it something spiritual or something physical? What do you believe? Why? Is this simply a matter of personal opinion or is this something that can be proven? If it can be proven, why is this subject surrounded by so much controversy?

Time and eternity are one.
D. T. Suzuki

# 5

# Are Human Beings Essentially Good or Evil?

Some religions believe that humans are born with a sinful nature and others believe that humans are born pure, but can become evil. Are we all born with a sinful nature that has to be cleansed and set right, or are we born pure and through learned behavior and circumstances become sinful or evil? Is everything black and white or do we all have both good and evil inside of us? Is everything dualistic as in the Tao philosophy of yin and yang? What is the driving force behind your beliefs on this subject?

All know the way, few actually walk it.
Bodhidharma

# 6

# What is Love?

Is love a spiritual force or nothing more than an emotion? Love is a very powerful thing, but what exactly is love? You can't touch it or see it, but we can see the effects of it. Is love an actual energy or force? Where does it come from? What causes it? Is love eternal or does it come and go? Is there such a thing as unconditional love or never-ending love?

Love in its essence is spiritual fire.
Emanuel Swedenborg

# 7

# Are You a Moral Person?

What does it mean to be a moral person? Who determines what is moral and what is not? Does God determine morality or is morality a cultural norm which stems from manmade laws and dictates? Why does morality differ from region to region in our world? What, if anything, changes your feeling regarding your personal morals? Has your morality changed over the years? How? Why?

The growth of moral virtues
depends upon one's self.
Nagarjuna

# 8

# Do You Believe in Situational Ethics?

Do you believe in absolute right and wrong or in situational ethics? Do your ethical standards change according to the situation at hand or are they permanently set in stone? Is right always right, and wrong always wrong, or does it depend on the situation? Is killing always a "sin" to you? What about in times of war? What about in self-defense? Is it wrong to lie? Cheat? Steal? Is there a situation in which you would consider these things to be acceptable? What would it be? Why? Should the situation affect your ethical standards?

Hold yourself responsible for a higher
standard than anyone else expects of you.
Never excuse yourself.
Henry Ward Beecher

# 9

# Are You a
# Good Person or a Bad Person?

What is a "good person" or a "bad person?" What determines this label? Your actions? Your heart? Your family? Who determines what is good or bad? In some countries a person is considered a "good person" if he kills his daughter or sister for having premarital sex. In the United States this person would be considered a murderer. So how do you know if you are truly a "good person" or a "bad person?" What is the difference between the two? Can a "good person" do bad things without becoming a "bad person?" Can a "bad person" do good things and become a "good person?" Do actions determine the kind of person you are or is it something else? What do you believe?

The number of people in possession of any
criteria for discriminating between
good and evil is very small.
T. S. Eliot

# 10

# Is the Death Penalty Moral?

Do you believe that killing someone for his actions is moral? Is it ever right to kill another human being? Is so, when? Why? Is the death penalty meant to be a punishment or a deterrent for others? Is it barbaric or a justified consequence for inappropriate actions? Is it the most efficient way to deter crime or are there better ways available to us? Is the death penalty an easier punishment for the criminal than a lifetime of hard labor? If you were the criminal, which punishment had you rather have, the death penalty or a lifetime of hard labor? Which punishment better serves our society? Why?

Let the punishment of criminals be useful.
Voltaire

# 11

# Should People be Able to Choose How They Die?

Is assisted suicide ethical? Should it be legal? Why or why not? If your loved one were dying slowly and painfully, would you help them on their journey if he or she requested your help? Should this be a personal decision or our government's decision? Why do you think we have a law against assisted suicide? How did other cultures in the past look at this issue? What, if anything, has changed where this is concerned? If you were terminally sick and in pain, would you want someone to help you leave your body or would you want to wait for nature to takes its course? What do you believe? Why?

Is freedom anything else than
the right to live as we wish.
Epictetus

# 12

# Should Illegal Drugs be Legalized?

Do you believe that illegal drugs should be legalized? Why are drugs illegal? Who should decide which drugs should be illegal and which drugs should be legal? Why? Are our drug laws effective? Is there a better way to control drug use? Why are tobacco and alcohol use legal, but marijuana use illegal? Are they really that different? How? Is the use of illegal drugs immoral? If so, would it still be immoral to use drugs if they were legal? Why or why not? Who determines morality? Was it immoral to drink alcohol during prohibition? If so, why is it not immoral to drink alcohol now, or is it? Is this something that should be legislated or should each individual decide what should or should not be put into his or her body? What do you think? Why?

Each man must for himself alone
decide what is right and what is wrong.
Mark Twain

# 13

# Is Public Profanity Acceptable?

Do you think that public profanity is acceptable? What does profanity say, if anything, about the person who is speaking? Does it bother you? Why or why not? If nothing is wrong with profanity, why is it considered inappropriate in certain situations or places? If there is something wrong with profanity, why do we hear it practically everywhere today? Do our words really matter? What do you believe? Why?

Behave to everyone as if you were receiving a great guest; do not do to others what you would not wish done to yourself.
Confucius

# 14

# Should Humans be Cloned?

Should human beings be cloned? Why or why not? Is cloning ethically moral? If you think humans should not be cloned, would you change your mind if cloning humans enabled scientists to cure diseases such as cancer or aids? Would cloned humans be "real" human beings? Would they have a soul? What is the basis of your belief concerning this subject? Is your belief based on facts or fear? Are there limits to how far science should go or is all knowledge meant to be explored?

There is a time when we must firmly choose
the course we will follow, or the relentless
drift of events will make the decision for us.
Herbert B. Prochnow

# 15

# Is Gambling Wrong?

Is it wrong to gamble? If it is, why is it legal to gamble in several states? If it is not wrong, why is it still illegal in many states? What makes gambling right or wrong? Is it only the laws of the land that determine if something is right or wrong, or are things inherently right or wrong? Is gambling right or wrong? Should someone else be able to dictate to you what you can and cannot do with your own money? If gambling is wrong, why does our government run lotteries? Aren't lotteries gambling? Does the amount of money gambled determine whether gambling is right or wrong? Why or why not? What do you think? Why?

What folly is it to play a game which you
can lose incomparably more than you can win.
Francesco Guicciardini

# Character Traits and Virtues

Because a human being
is so malleable, whatever one
cultivates is what one becomes.
Lao Tzu

# 16

# What does Integrity Mean to You?

If someone has integrity, what does that mean to you? How does someone with integrity act? How do they think? How do you know if someone has integrity? Is integrity important? Why or why not? Do you think integrity is a rare character trait or do you believe that most people have integrity? Are there degrees of integrity or is integrity an absolute trait? Would you prefer to deal with someone with this character trait or does it really matter? Why or why not? How much integrity do you have?

For when moral value is considered, the concern is not the actions, which are seen, but rather with their inner principles, which are not seen.
Immanuel Kant

# 17

# Are You Honorable?

What is honor? How do you define honor? Who determines what honor is? Who determines whether or not you have honor? You? Your family? Your friends? Society as a whole? Does honor matter to you? Why or why not? Can honor mean one thing to one person and something entirely different to someone else or is honor a universal trait which means the same everywhere? What do you think? What is your belief based on?

Our own heart, and not other men's
opinion, form our true honor.
Samuel Coleridge

# 18

# Are You a Racist?

Do you look at the heart or the skin color? What is more important to you someone's character or the color of someone's skin? Is race the first thing that you notice when meeting someone of a different race for the first time? Do you believe that there are many different races or one race - the human race? Would you want your son or daughter to marry someone of a different race? Does it matter what race? Would you get romantically involved with someone of a different race? Would it matter which race? Be honest...what do you really believe? Why?

A human being is a part of the whole that we call the universe, a part limited in time and space.
Albert Einstein

# 19

# Are You Honest?

How important is honesty to you? Are you honest all the time or just when it is suitable to your purpose or when it doesn't really matter? Are there times when you believe it is better to be dishonest? If so, when? Why? Is honesty always the best policy? What if your life or the life of someone else depended on a lie, would it then be okay to be dishonest? Why or why not? Is honesty dependant on the situation or should everyone always be honest? What do you really believe? Are you honest? To what degree?

Things are often spoke and seldom meant.
Shakespeare

## 20

# What is the True Test
# of Someone's Character?

How do you test someone's character? How do you really know if someone has an upstanding character or not? Can you ever really know what is in someone else's heart? Can you truly trust other people? How do you know for sure, or can you know for sure? Do you have anyone in your life that you can trust 100 percent? Who? How sure are you? Can people really trust you 100 percent? Why or why not? How long does it take for someone to prove their good character to you? What do you look at to determine someone's character? Why?

Our true character silently underlies
all our words and actions, as the
granite underlies the other strata.
Henry David Thoreau

# 21

# Are You Prejudiced?

Would you invite a serial killer or a rapist into your home for Christmas dinner? No? Then you are prejudice against serial killers and rapists. Everyone is prejudiced toward someone or something. What are your prejudices? Why do you have these prejudices in your life? How did they develop? Do your prejudices help you or hinder you in your life? In what ways? Are your prejudices justified or do you need to change them or get rid of them? How can you change them or remove them? Think about it.

There is very little difference between
one man and another; but what little
difference there is, is very important.
William James

## 22

# Should You Judge Others?

Do you judge others? Are you judgmental concerning their actions? Their lifestyle? Their speech? Their looks? Should you be? Why or why not? Does someone's lifestyle or the way that he or she dresses tell you who that person really is? Does it tell you anything about them? If so, what? Can you judge a book by its cover? What about a person? What really determines who a person is inside? If you judge others, what standards do you use? Why?

Faces we see, hearts we know not.
Spanish Proverb

# 23

# What Character Traits are Important to You?

What character traits do you admire most in other people? Are those character traits a part of your life? What character traits do you most respect in yourself? Why are these character traits important to you? What do these character traits say about you? What character traits would you like to change or replace in your life? Why? How important is your character? How important is your reputation? Does your character and your reputation mesh? Why or why not?

Virtue is more clearly shown in the performance of fine actions than in the nonperformance of base ones.
Aristotle

## 24

# How Important are Manners?

Do manners really matter to you? Do you try hard to exhibit good manners at all times or are you too lax in this area of your life? Why do manners matter? What do good manners actually say about you? Do they say anything at all about you? Where do manners come from? Are manners written in stone or do they change with the times? Why? Who determines what is rude or what are bad manners? What do bad manners say about someone? What do you think? Why?

Consideration of others is
the basis of a good life.
Confucius

# 25

# What Would You Do?

What would you do if you knew no one else would ever find out about your actions? This is the real test of your character. Would you lie? Cheat? Steal? Would the fact that nobody would ever find out about your actions change your attitude towards the way that you behave at all? Would it change your actions concerning your integrity and honesty? What about your sexual activities or using illegal drugs? Are you living your life as a hypocrite? What determines your morality, your character or what others may think of your actions? Is your reputation simply a facade or do you take your character seriously?

Wise people, even though all laws were abolished, would still lead the same life.
Aristophanes

# 26

# What Could You Do?

What could you do if you had to? If you lost your family could you make it on your own in this world? Could you kill someone to save your family? What about to save yourself in a self-defense situation? Could you survive in the wilderness for days? Just what are you prepared to do and what are you not prepared to do? How prepared are you for life's unexpected adventures? How could you be better prepared? Should you be better prepared? Are there things that you absolutely will not do? If so, what are they? What determines what you are and are not willing to do?

Courage is grace under pressure.
Ernest Hemingway

# 27

# What Would You do for 10 Million Dollars?

What would you do for 10 million dollars? Would the prospect of this much money change your perspective? Would it change your attitudes concerning what you are or are not willing to do? Would you do anything to get your hands on that kind of money? Would you commit murder? Would you break the law in some other way? Would you turn your back on your friends? Does this much money even tempt you at all? If 10 million dollars doesn't tempt you, is there a certain amount that would? Be honest with yourself. How strong are your moral beliefs?

Few men have the virtue to
withstand the highest bidder.
George Washington

# 28

# What if You Were Dying?

If you knew that you were going to die in one month, how would you live your last month on this earth? Why? Why aren't you living this way now? What is stopping you from doing what you really want to right now? Do you have to be dying to really start living? Do you really know that you won't die in one month? Are any of us promised any certain amount of time on this planet? Should you live every moment to its fullest or should you sacrifice now for later pleasures? What do you think? Why?

This is not a dress rehearsal. This is it.
Tom Cunningham

# Money
# and
# Success

Too many people overvalue
what they are not and
undervalue what they are.
Malcolm S. Forbes

## 29

# What are Your Priorities?

What are your priorities in life? Is your main priority making money? Is it your family? Is it your leisure time? How do you know what your priorities are? Do you have priorities or are you just aimlessly going through the motions of life, doing the same things day after day? What needs to be your main priority in order to have the kind of life that you want to have? Do you need to change your priorities in order to get your life on track? If so, in what way? How do you know whether or not you need to get your priorities straight?

Live mindful of how brief your life is.
Horace

# 30

# How Should You Choose a Career?

Do you believe that you should choose a career based on money or based on what interests you? Which decision do you think makes for a happier life? Why? How important is money to your career choice? Do you think that having more money will make you happier? If so, how do you know? What if you are wrong? Is it ever too late to start a new career? If so, what is the "cut-off" age for changing careers? Why? Have any other people successfully changed careers past that "cut-off" age? What determines this deadline? What are the consequences for making the wrong decision concerning your career?

Whenever it is possible, a boy should
choose some occupation which he should
do even if he did not need the money.
William Lyon Phelps

# 31

# What if Money was no Problem?

How important is money to you? Do you have your priorities in the right order? What would you do if money was no problem and you had all the money that you could ever need or want? How would you spend your time? Where would you go? What would you do? Would you have a career? Would it be the same one that you currently have? Why is this not your career now? Are you living your life in the present or waiting to win the lotto or retire before you really start living?

Everybody who lives dies.
But not everybody who dies has lived.
Dhaggi Ramanashi

# 32

# What is True Prosperity?

What things make up true prosperity? Is prosperity all about money or does it go much further than monetary things? What is true prosperity to you? What all does it involve? Money? Health? Family? Happiness? Other things? How do you become prosperous? What determines how prosperous you are? Are you trying to keep up with the "Jones" or do you decide for yourself what defines your own prosperity? Think about this.

True prosperity has a spiritual basis.
Catherine Ponder

# 33

# What is True Success?

How do you know that someone is successful? Does it have to do with money? How much money does it take to be considered a success? Who determines this amount? Does being a success involve more than money? If so, what does it entail? Can someone be a success in life and not be financially well off? How? What is true success to you? Why? Who determines whether or not someone is a success? Is success something that is universal or does success vary from person to person, and place to place?

There is only one success to be
able to live life in your own way.
Christopher Morley

# 34

## Is it Important to be Self-Sufficient?

What does being self-sufficient mean to you? Are you self-sufficient? In what ways are you self-sufficient? How do you know? If you aren't self-sufficient, who or what do you depend on? In what ways are you dependent? What would happen if someone or something that you depend on were suddenly no longer available for you? Do you think that you could survive if the people and things that you depend on were suddenly no longer available to you? Do you know how to provide your own food and water for your basic needs? Do you think it is important to be self-sufficient? Why or why not?

Never depend on anyone except yourself.
La Fontaine

# 35

# How Will You Live When You Retire?

Are you planning ahead for your retirement? How do you plan on living when you retire? Is your whole life already centered on your retirement? Are you sacrificing the present for the future or are you living life to its fullest while you also plan for the future? Where do you plan on living? Do you believe that your life is coming to an end when you retire or is it just the next chapter of a vibrant life that has been lived to the fullest? What is your attitude toward your golden years?

We are always getting ready
to live but never living.
Ralph Waldo Emerson

## 36

# Is Saving Money Important to You?

Do you spend every dime that you make or is saving money important to you? Do you really believe that saving money is important? Why or why not? If you do believe you should save money, do you save enough each month? How do you know? Why do you believe that saving money is important? Are you motivated to save money out of fear of the future or out of excitement for the future? Can you save money and still live life fully in the present? Why or why not? How much money do you need to save to feel secure? Are you sure this is enough to provide for you need later in life? How do you know?

If you keep adding little by little,
it will soon become a big heap.
Hesiod

## 37

# What do You Think about Debt?

Do you live on credit? What do you believe concerning debt? Is debt necessary or do you avoid it altogether? Does it bother you to be in debt either financially or in any other way? Why or why not? Do you understand how compound interest works and how much financial debt can cost you in interest? Is debt unavoidable in our society? Why or why not? Do you consider repaying favors a debt much like repaying money? Do you believe in lending money or other things to others? Why?

The cost of a thing is the amount of what I will call life which is required to be exchanged for it, immediately or in the long run.
Henry David Thoreau

# Politics
# and
# Government

High beings of deep universal
virtue work unassertively. They
help all people, yet people are
barely aware of their existence.
Lao Tzu

# 38

# Are You Conservative or Liberal?

How do you classify yourself politically? Are you a conservative or a liberal? What determines if you are a conservative or a liberal? Can you actually classify yourself as either of these? Are you sure? Why or why not? What is the main difference in the two? Do you believe that everyone is one or the other, or are most people balanced somewhere in the middle? Are these your only two choices or are these simply labels created by the media? What do you think?

All politics are based on the
indifference of the majority.
James Reston

# 39

# Should Each Vote Count Equally?

Should everyone's vote count equally or should some people's votes hold more weight than other people's votes? Should someone who is informed and intelligent have their vote count more than someone who has no idea what is going on? Why or why not? Do you think that everyone makes an informed decision when it comes to voting or do they vote with a lack of knowledge concerning the issues? Should our ballets be printed in other languages besides English? Why? Do you think that everyone has an equal amount at stake when it comes to our elections or do some people have more on the line? Why? Do you think that everyone's vote counts equally in our current system?

In proportion as the structure of government gives force to public opinion, it is essential that public opinion should be enlightened.
George Washington

# 40

# Is Our Legal System Just?

Do you believe that our legal system is just? Is it unbiased and fair? Would you bet your life on it? How has our legal system changed your life? Are you more fearful of being involved in a lawsuit? Has our legal system cost you more in insurance? Has it helped you? Does money play a part in our legal system? How? If you were accused of a serious crime and had a chance to leave the country, would you? Why or why not? Do you think that getting a just verdict depends more on getting a good lawyer or being innocent? What if you can't afford a good lawyer? Would this change your attitude? Why or why not?

The people's good is the highest law.
Cicero

# 41

# Is War Ever Justified?

What, if anything, justifies killing thousands of human beings? If you believe that war is sometimes justified, when is it necessary? Why? What makes it a necessary part of our world? What would happen if we refused to fight? Does it have to be this way? Is violence just an unavoidable part of life or is violence never justified? What do you believe? Why? Who should make decisions concerning war? Are these people trustworthy? Should war be defensive only or is pre-emptive war justified? If you believe that war is never justified, how would aggressive, rogue nations be kept from bringing about another Holocaust?

There will never be peace between nations...
until there is true peace in the souls of men.
Black Elk

## 42

# Are You Politically Correct?

Are you politically correct or do you say exactly what's on your mind? Is it important that everything that you say be completely neutral so you don't offend anyone? Is this the kind of country that our founding fathers had in mind? Did our forefathers vision a country where citizens have to censor each thought for political correctness? Do you believe political correctness is needed because of our diverse population? Are you under an obligation to make sure that your beliefs and speech fit into the norm so neither offends anyone else? Is this true freedom or a form of intimidation? What do you think? Why?

Liberty is meaningless where the right to utter one's thoughts and opinions has ceased to exist.
Frederick Douglas

# 43

# What is Your Duty to Your Country?

Do you have a duty to your country? If so, what is it? What does it entail? Why do you have a duty to your country? Do you have a greater duty to yourself and your beliefs, or to your country? Why? If you moved to another country, would you have a duty to that country or would you still have a duty to your original country? Should your country come before your family? Your religion? Your integrity? In what order do you place these things? Why? What do you think?

Power must never be trusted without a check.
John Adams

## 44

# Does Our Education System Work?

Does our system of education work? Are our children receiving a good education? Do you think that our children are receiving as good of an education as your grandparents received? Why or why not? Do you really know what is going on in your child's school? How important is your child's education to you? If it is important, why are teachers' salaries so low? Should this be changed? Why or why not? Do you approve of school vouchers? Why or why not? Should the government be in charge of your child's education or should you be able to make those decisions as a parent? What do you think?

To educate a man in mind and not in moral
is to educate a menace to society.
Theodore Roosevelt

# Spirituality and Religion

There is only one religion though there are a hundred versions of it.
George Bernard Shaw

## 45

# Are Religion and Spirituality the Same?

Are religion and spirituality the same or two distinct categories? If they are different, how so? Where does spirituality come from? Where does religion come from? Which is more important? Why? Can one exist without the other or are they dependent on each other? Is religion good? Is spirituality good? What are the good points and bad points of each of these two? Which do you relate to more? Why? Is religion man-made or did religion originate with God? What about spirituality? What is the purpose of religion? What do you believe? Why?

In quarreling about the shadow,
we often lose the substance.
Aesop

## 46

# Is There a God?

Do you believe that God is real? How do you know? Why do you believe in God? Do you believe in God because of your religious upbringing or because of your personal experiences? What evidence supports your belief? Are you sure that you believe in God or is this just what you are expected to believe? If you believe that God does not exist, how do you know? Why do you believe this? Do you just like being the rebel and going against the grain, or do you really believe there is no God? Would you still believe this if you knew that you were going to die tonight? Why? What if you are wrong?

Refusing to choose is a choice;
disbelief is a belief.
Bohdi Sanders

## 47

# What Religion is God?

We have many religions on our earth. Each one has its own Holy Scriptures, rituals, and beliefs. But what religion is God? Does God really favor one religion over another? Is God really interested in our religions or is God only interested in spirituality? Do all religions come from the same source or is there only one "true" religion? If there is only one true religion, who or what determines which one is true? Is organized religion what God had in mind for the human race? What is your evidence? How do you know?

Your mind cannot possibly understand God.
Your heart already knows.
Emmanuel

## 48

# What Happens When You Die?

What happens to you when you die? Are you just dead and no longer exist, or do you have a spirit that lives forever? Are you reincarnated again and again, or do you go to Heaven or Hell? Do you roam the earth as a free spirit or do you have a choice? Does the prospect of death raise feelings of fear in you, or are you comfortable with your beliefs of life after death? How sure are you? Is this important to you? Have you taken the time to think about your beliefs on this subject? What do you base your beliefs on?

There is no death.
Only a change of worlds.
Chief Seattle

## 49

# Do You Believe that Scripture is the "Word of God?"

Do you believe that the scriptures are the divine word of God or are they only a good source of wise sayings and history? Many people believe that the Bible is word for word, the "Word of God" and that it speaks directly to them personally. Others believe that the Bible is just a book of history and myths. Do you believe that Jonah actually lived in the stomach of a whale for three days or that Noah put a male and a female of every living creature on his ark? Are these stories fact or fiction? What about the Vedas or the Dhammapada or the many other scriptures throughout the world, are they true? What do you think? Why?

Most of the world's people
worship the offspring, while one who
is spiritually mature embraces the Source.
Lao Tzu

# 50

# Is There a Real "Devil?"

Do you believe that there is a real being known as "Satan" or "the Devil?" Does this being really exist or is Satan just a metaphor for evil in general? If he does exist, what do you think his purpose is? Why would an omnipotent God create such an evil being? Does he have a purpose in this world? What is the driving force behind Satanism if Satan is not real? What do you think? What is your belief based on? If Satan is not real, where does evil come from? The heart of men? The mind? Negative energy? What do you think?

The only thing necessary for the triumph of evil
is for good men to do nothing.
Edmond Burke

# 51

# What Are You?

Do you believe that you are spirit, mind and body or do you not believe that you have a spirit? Are you a spiritual being having a human experience or are you a physical being that is having a spiritual experience? Is there actually a separation of the three parts or are you just a body? If you do believe that you are spirit, mind and body, which of these is the most important to you? Why? Do you live like you believe this? Why or why not? If you do believe that you are a spirit or have a spirit, how do you know? What exactly do you believe a spirit is?

Faith is believing what we cannot prove.
Alfred Lord Tennyson

## 52

# Do You Believe that Heaven is a Real Place?

Do you believe in Heaven? Is it a real place? If so, how does someone get to Heaven? Where is Heaven? Is your place in Heaven predetermined? Is it a gift from God or do you have to earn it? Do you get to go to Heaven by believing in God? In Jesus? In Buddha? In Muhammad? Can a murderer go to Heaven if he repents at the last minute or is he forever held responsible for his crimes? Where does someone go if he does not go to Heaven? How do you know? What is your belief based on?

No matter what road I travel, I'm going home.
Shinso

# 53

# Does Hell Really Exist?

Is there an actual place called Hell? Did God create Hell to torment people who have made poor life choices or for anyone who does not follow specific religious requirements? Is Hell only for demons and Satan himself? If someone goes to Hell, is all hope lost? Can they call on God to help them or is it too late? Is Hell eternal torture for those who end up there? Is Hell only a metaphor used in scriptures? Is there any evidence? What is your belief based on? If there is a place called Hell, where is it? Where did it come from? How do you know?

No man can be ignorant that he must die,
nor be sure that he may not this very day.
Cicero

## 54

# Is God Omnipotent?

Is God all-powerful? Is God everywhere all the time? Does He actually control everything that happens in your life? In the world? In the universe? Does He have time to really be concerned with you and your problems? If He is in control of everything, why do bad things happen to good people? Does God control everything or does human free will control things and God simply manage damage control? If God is omnipotent, why does God allow evil to exist instead of removing all evil from the world? What do you think? Why?

The universe is the body of one Being.
Lao Tzu

# 55

# What is God?

If you believe that God does exists, what is He? Does the pronoun "He" accurately fit God? Is God an actual being or is God pure energy? Is God pure light or is He pure love? How did God come to be God? Where did He come from? Does anyone really know? Can you know God? How? How do you know? What do you really believe?

For what is God?
He is the soul of the Universe.
Seneca

# The
# Metaphysical
# World

We must walk in balance
on the earth, a foot in the
spirit and a foot in the physical.
Lynn Andrews

# 56

# Are There Other Worlds Out There?

Is Earth the only planet in the universe that maintains intelligent life or is there intelligent life in other parts of the universe? Could there be an alternate universe? What about a parallel universe? Does Earth host the only intelligent life across millions of light years or are there life forms out there that are asking themselves this same question? What do you believe? If Earth is the only planet that maintains intelligent life, what makes Earth so special? Is there something inherently special about our planet or about human beings? If so, what is it?

All are but parts of one stupendous whole,
whose body nature is, and God the soul.
Alexander Pope

## 57

# Are Psychics Real?

Can some people really tell your future? Can some people contact your dead friends and relatives, or read your mind? Are people who claim to be psychic just cons or do they really possess supernatural powers? If they are real, are they just gifted or are they using human powers that are available to every human being who is willing to develop these powers? Does everyone have a sixth sense? How do you know? Where does this ability come from? Can it be developed? What does the evidence show?

Intuition is a spiritual faculty and does not explain, but simply points the way.
Florence Scovel Shinn

## 58

# Do You Believe in Ghosts?

Do ghosts actually exist? Do you become a ghost when you die? How do you explain the many people who claim to have seen a ghost or who have claimed that their home haunted by a ghost? If ghosts do exist, are they all around us at all times or are they only found in certain haunted houses and cemeteries? If they exist, are they dangerous or just mischievous? Are ghosts lost spirits or a form of spiritual energy? What are they? Where do they come from? What do you believe? Why?

Millions of spiritual creatures walk this earth
unseen, both when we wake, and when we sleep.
John Milton

# 59

# Do Auras Really Exist?

Does everyone have an aura? Can people really see auras around your body? If so, what does your aura show about you? Is there any scientific evidence to support your belief? Does everything have an aura or just human beings? What about chakras or an energy field? What do you think? If auras do not exist, why do so many people believe in them? What does Kirkland Photography show? If Kirkland Photography does not show auras, what cause the colors around the body shown in these photographs? If auras do exist, what is the purpose of them?

Trust the instinct to the end,
though you can render no reason.
Ralph Waldo Emerson

# 60

# How do You Explain Mind Over Matter?

Is mind over matter real or some sort of hoax? How do people bend forks, knives, etc. using their mind? Is this some sort of illusion or is there more to our minds than meets the eye? If mind over matter is real, do you believe it is something that should be explored and used or is it something to fear and stay away from? Why? What is your opinion based on? Can your mind be developed to a much greater extent than men has ever imagined? If so, how?

What mortals see are delusions.
True vision is detached from seeing.
Bodhidharma

# 61

# Do You Believe in Magic?

Do you believe that magic is real or is it simply a myth? Are there really people out there who have magical powers? Are witches simply people who are living in a fantasy world or can they really conjure magical spells? If magic is real, is it good or evil? How do you know? If magic is not real, why do so many people seem to believe in it? Is magic simply directing the power of your thoughts or something more? What do you think? Where did the concept of magic come from? Why do many people believe that magic is evil? Are these beliefs valid? Where did these beliefs originate? What was the purpose behind these beliefs? Were there agendas behind these beliefs or are they valid?

The most beautiful thing we can experience is the mysterious.
Albert Einstein

# 62

# Do Your Thoughts Have Power?

Do your thoughts really matter? Do your thoughts have power? Do they have power to cause certain things to happen or to manifest certain things in your life? What are thoughts? Are they energy? Are they forces? Where do thoughts comes from? Is it important to control your thoughts or does it not matter as long as you control your actions? Does it matter if your thoughts are positive or negative? Do they really affect your body or your life? If so, do you consciously make an effort to control your thoughts throughout the day? Why or why not? Is there any evidence to support your beliefs on this subject?

Actions are made of thoughts.
The Upanishads

# The
# Earth

The world is one percent good,
one percent bad, ninety-eight
percent neutral. It can go one way
or the other, depending on which
side is pushing. This is why what
individuals do is important.
Lao Tzu

# 63

# How was the Earth Formed?

Do you believe in the Big Bang Theory or in Creationism? Did our world evolve accidentally or was every small detail perfectly planned? If our earth was created, why was it created? What is the purpose of this incredible creation? Do you believe one of the many creation stories or in a scientific theory concerning this issue? What do you believe? Why?

Truth rest with God alone.
Yiddish Proverb

# 64

# Has Man Destroyed the Earth?

Have we gone too far in polluting our planet? Can the damage that we have done to the earth be reversed? Should we even try or care about this issue? Does recycling actually help our planet? In what way? Should we ban the use of poisons on crops? Do these pesticides and herbicides really harm the earth or our water supply? If so, why are we still allowing them to be used? What, if anything, will it take for you to reach a point of demanding environmental changes? Where do you draw the line?

The nation that destroys its soil destroys itself.
Franklin Delano Roosevelt

# 65

# Is Overpopulation a Problem?

How many people can the earth sustain? Is there a limit? Is overpopulation the problem or are greed and our current lifestyle the problem? Do we have enough food on this planet for everyone or is there really a food shortage? Is this a physical problem or an economic problem? If overpopulation is a problem, what should be done about it? What do you believe? What does the evidence show? If overpopulation is a problem, who should stop procreating? Why? Are some people more important than others? Why or why not?

The earth is given as common stock
for man to labor and live on.
Thomas Jefferson

# 66

# Are We Running Out of Water?

Is there a water shortage on the earth? Is the earth's fresh water supply running dangerously low? What about "pure" water? Does the current use of pesticides and insecticides endanger our supply of fresh, clean drinking water? If so, what should be done about it? Is our municipal water supply safe or do the chemicals used to purify it cause danger for humans? Is bottled water a scam or a necessity in these times? What do you think? What does the evidence show?

Conservation is a state of harmony
between man and land.
Aldo Leopold

# 67

# Do Animals have Rights?

Do animals have rights? If so, what rights do they have? Who determines whether or not they have any rights? Are humans abusing their rights? How? Is it right to raise animals for food? If it is not, are you a vegetarian? What about raising animals for fur? Is this ethical? Why or why not? Do certain animals have more rights than others? If so, what determines which animals how higher rights? Does a dog have more rights to be treated humanely than a pig or a cow? Why or why not? What do you believe? Why?

Everything is sacred.
Black Elk

# 68

## Do Animals have a Soul?

Do animals have a soul? Do they feel emotions? Can they love each other or humans? Do animals communicate? Can animals really understand humans? Why can't animals talk? What makes us so different from animals? What happens to animals when they die? How do you know? What are your beliefs on this subject based on?

An animal's eyes have the power
to speak a great language.
Martin Buber

# 69

## Is the Earth in Danger?

Is the earth in danger of being destroyed? What affects would nuclear war have on the earth? Would the earth recover from such a war? Are we in danger from a meteor crashing into the earth? What affects would this have on the earth? If the earth or part of the earth was destroyed, would it cease to exist or would it recreate itself? What would happen if something pollutes our oceans to a point that they cannot sustain life? How would this affect humans? Is this a possibility? What do you think?

From a grain of sand to a
great mountain, all is sacred.
Peter Blue Cloud

# Health

# Issues

The future is
purchased by the present.
French Proverb

# 70

# Are You Healthy?

Are you healthy? Do you watch your diet? How strictly? Do you get regular exercise? How often? How often do you really push yourself to the limit? How often do you get sick? Why? Are you mentally healthy? Do you learn new things and use your mind? Are you emotionally stable or are you very moody? Do you have a positive outlook or are you a negative person? What about spiritually, are you spiritually healthy? Do you participate in exercises that increase your spiritual health? Is your health balanced spirit, mind and body?

Life is not merely living, but living in health.
Martial

# 71

# Do Your Thoughts Affect Your Health?

Many alternative health practitioners state that your thoughts affect your health. It is suggested that negative thoughts and feelings of hate and unforgiveness can adversely affect your physical health. What do you think? Is there any real evidence? If you do believe that this is true, how carefully do you try to control your thoughts? Can you control your thoughts? Is there really a mind/body connection? If your thoughts are connected to your health, can you use your thoughts to heal your physical body? If there is not a mind/ body connection, how do you explain the placebo affect? What do you think?

You are today where your
Thoughts have brought you; you will be
tomorrow where your thoughts take you.
James Lane Allen

# 72

# Can the Body Heal Itself?

Is your body designed to heal itself or are you dependent on modern medicine for your health? Is holistic health care that relies on natural cures, along with the body's natural healing abilities, reliable? If you believe that the body can heal itself, why do you take medicine? If you had cancer, would you trust your life to alternative cures that focus on detoxification of your body, or would you depend on modern treatments such as chemotherapy and radiation? Why? If you believe that the body can heal itself, why do you go to the doctor? Do you really believe in natural health care or do you merely want to believe in it because it is hip?

It is the mind that rules the body.
Sojourner Truth

# 73

# Do You Believe in Energy Healing?

Can holistic practitioners use energy to heal others? Does everything from rocks to humans have a subtle energy field? Is reiki, the art of healing with energy, real or does it rely on the placebo effect? What evidence is your opinion based on? Is energy "magical" or is it scientific? What do you believe? Why? Do people really have auras? If so, do those auras indicate the state of someone's health? What does the evidence show?

Prayer, like radium, is a luminous
and self-generating form of energy.
Dr. Alexis Carrel

# 74

# Should You Be a Vegetarian?

Are human beings meant to be vegetarians or meat eaters? How do you know? Is your body designed to eat only fruits and vegetables or is it designed to eat whatever you decide to feed it? What evidence backs up your opinion on this matter? Are you sure? Is it safe and healthy to be a vegetarian? Is it ethical to eat meat? Does right and wrong even have anything to do with this issue, or is this purely a personal choice? What do you think?

The destiny of countries depends
on the way they feed themselves.
Anthelme Brillat-Savarin

## 75

# Do You Trust the Medical Profession?

Does your doctor have your best interest at heart or is he too busy making money and dealing with paperwork to take a personal interest in your health? Is the drug industry interested in what is best for your health or is this industry only interested in making profits? If the drug industry is interested in improving your health, why doesn't it test natural cures such as herbs and nutritional supplements? Can you really trust the "experts?" Is alternative medicine a viable option for you? Why or why not? What does the evidence show?

Trust, but verify.
Russian Proverb

# 76

# What if You had Cancer?

If you were diagnosed with cancer, what type of treatment would you want? Chemotherapy? Natural holistic alternatives? What steps could you take now to ensure against the possibility of developing cancer? Which type of medical practitioner would you be confident going to for treatment? Why? Do you believe that you have to get treatment, or is your body able to heal itself given the proper nutrition? Does your mind play a part in healing your body of cancer? How? How do you know? How would a diagnosis of cancer change your life? Would it make you take your life more seriously? If so, why aren't you taking your life this serious now?

The joyfulness of a man prolongs his days.
Book of Psalms

# 77

## Is Restaurant Food Safe?

Do you have confidence in the food that you order from a restaurant? Do you feel that the employees are people that you can trust with your health? Do you feel that these people are interested in your health and well-being? Do you think that this food is conducive to good health? If not, why do you eat it? Will you eat at most any restaurant or are you selective? How do you know if you can trust a restaurant? What is your determining factor? What about the food in school cafeterias? Are your children getting the kind of nutrition that they need? Are you sure? If not, why do you allow them to eat this food? Are you sacrificing your children's health for convenience or do you truly trust the quality of food in our schools? How important is the quality of the food that you put into your body to your health?

One cannot think well, love well,
or sleep well, if one has not dined well.
Virginia Woolf

# 78

# Do You have a Living Will?

Do you have a living will? Would you want to be kept alive by a machine or would you rather pass on when your body can no longer sustain life on its own? Why? Do you want to make this choice or do you want to leave this choice up to someone else? Is it fair to have someone else make this choice for you? Why or why not? Who would you trust to make this decision for you if you decide not to make it for yourself? Why would you choose to be kept alive by a machine? Why would you choose not to be on life support? Think about it.

Old and young, we are all on our last cruise.
Robert Louis Stevenson

# Relationships and Sex

Every pebble in the brook secretly
thinks itself a precious stone.
Japanese Proverb

# 79

# What Makes a Strong Marriage?

What factors are involved in a strong marriage? Why? Who do you know that has a strong marriage? What traits do they exhibit? Do you expect your marriage to last forever? Why or why not? Do you believe in "soul mates?" Do you believe that there is one special person for everyone or do you believe that there are many people that are compatible for each other? Should a husband and wife have unconditional love?? What do you believe? Why?

When a match has equal partners,
then I fear not.
Aeschylus

# 80

# What are the Characteristics of a Good Parent?

What are the characteristics of a good parent? How do you know if you are a good parent or not? What factors do you use to evaluate whether or not you are a good parent? Your own judgment? How well liked you are? Your children's behavior? Who do you consider a good parent? Why? Do you consider your parents good parents? Why or why not? What are the most important characteristics of a good parent? Why? What would your children say? Are you a good parent? If not, how can you become a good parent? How important is it to be a good parent? If it is important, why is there so little emphasis put on how to be a good parent?

You are the bows from which your children are as living arrows sent forth.
Kahlil Gibran

# 81

# Do You Love Your Spouse Unconditionally?

Is your love unconditional? Is there even such a thing as unconditional love? Will you still love your spouse no matter what he or she does? Is there anything that would change your love for your spouse? Is so, what? Why? Do you express to your spouse that you love him or her unconditionally? How? Are you sure that he or she knows how you feel? How important is unconditional love? Why?

Love is blind.
Geoffrey Chaucer

# 82

# What is a Perfect Spouse?

What do you expect from your spouse? What does your spouse expect from you? Are your expectations realistic or are they influenced by Hollywood? Do you feel that you are living up to your spouse's expectations? Why or why not? Is your spouse living up to your expectations? Does your spouse know what your expectations or desires are? Why or why not? What are the traits of a "perfect" spouse? How do you know? If your relationship is not as good as you would like, how can you make it better? What do you think?

Treat people as if they were what they should be,
and you help them become what
they are capable of becoming.
Johann von Goethe

# 83

# Is Premarital Sex Moral?

Many people believe that people should not have sex before they are married. Others believe that it doesn't matter. What do you believe? Why? What is your belief based on? Health reasons? Spiritual reasons? Religious reasons? Something else? Is this your belief or someone else's belief? If you don't believe premarital sex is moral, what are your reasons? What makes it immoral? What if you are dedicated to your partner but just don't want to get married, would it still be immoral? Why? What would be the difference? What do you think? Why?

If you are standing upright,
don't worry if your shadow is crooked.
Chinese Proverb

# 84

# Is Sex a Spiritual Act?

Do you consider sex a spiritual act or a physical act, or is it a combination of the two? Many people consider sex to be a spiritual act. Tantric sex is considered to heighten spirituality. What do you think? Is sex purely for enjoyment? Is sex only for procreation? Is it meant to heighten your spirituality? Is it all of the above? What do you believe? Why? What do you base your belief on? Is this a personal decision or is it a universal constant? How do you know?

You mustn't force sex to do the work
of love or love to do the work of sex.
Mary McCarthy

85

# Would You Sleep with Someone for Money?

The immediate answer to this question for most people is "no," but let's take it a little further. Would you sleep with someone for $1,000? $10,000? $50,000? $100,000? $1 million? How about $10 million? Where do you draw the line? Is there any point at which you would change your mind about your original answer? Are you sure? Would it matter who the other person was? What if it were some good looking movie star making the offer? Would that influence your decision? Think about it.

Though the wind blows,
the mountain does not move.
Japanese Proverb

# 86

# Are All Sexual Acts Moral?

Are there any sexual acts that couples should not participate in or do you believe that all sexual acts are moral if both partners are willing? What determines if something between two adults is moral or immoral? What is perverted to you? What is your definition of perverted? Where do you draw the line between something being moral and immoral? Why do you feel this way? Is this anyone else's business besides the two people involved? Why or why not? If it is no one else's business, why do many states have laws against different sex acts? Is this something that the government should be involved in? Why or why not? What do you believe? What is your belief based on?

It is wisdom to believe the heart.
George Santayana

# 87

# Is Pornography Harmless Entertainment?

Do you believe that pornography is harmless entertainment or is it a dangerous and addicting form of exploitation? Should pornography be legal? Is it destructive to families and communities or is it simply harmless fun for couples and singles? What do you think? What is your belief based on? Is there any evidence to support your belief? Do you distinguish between "hard core" pornography and other forms of pornography? What about erotic "R" rated movies? Are these movies also pornography? Where do you draw the line or do you? Why? What do you think?

Highly evolved people have their
own conscience as pure law.
Lao Tzu

# 88

# Should Prostitution be Legal?

Is the "oldest profession" immoral and something that should be controlled legally or should people have the right to do whatever they wish with their bodies? Does prostitution hurt anyone? If so, who? How? Does it affect communities in a detrimental way? Does making prostitution illegal control it or slow it down, or does it simply cause it to move underground? What is the difference in prostitution and promiscuous sex, besides the exchange of money? What do you think? Why? Does the evidence support your belief?

Useless laws diminish the
authority of necessary ones.
French Proverb

# 89

# Is Homosexuality a Sexual Preference?

Do you believe that homosexuality is a sexual preference or is one born with homosexual tendencies? Does homosexuality have something to do with the chemical make-up of someone's mind and body, or is it simply a lifestyle choice? How do you know? Is there any scientific evidence concerning this? If it is a sexual preference, is that acceptable to you? Why or why not? What drives your opinion on this heated subject? What do you think?

God offers to every mind its choice
between truth and repose.
Ralph Waldo Emerson

# 90

# Are Computer Relationships Cheating?

Is having a relationship over the computer harmless or is it being unfaithful to your spouse or partner? Do you believe that flirting and talking intimately online is a form of cheating or is it just harmless fun? Do you think it is wrong? If so, why? Is it safe? Would your spouse or partner agree with your view on this subject? Is it something that you would want your spouse or partner to do behind your back? Why or why not? Are computer relationships real? Do people really develop feelings simply by communicating over the computer? What do you believe?

Good instincts usually tell you what to do
long before your head has figured it out.
Michael Burke

# 91

# How Important is Family to You?

How important is family to you? Do you only consider your immediate family relationships important or is extended family important to you also? Why? If you believe that family is important, how do you ensure that you have strong family ties? How important is spending time with your family? Do you feel that you spend enough time with your family? Why or why not? Where does your family rank among your priorities? If your family is important to you, how do you let them know this? Do they know how you feel? Why or why not? What could you do to make your relationship with your family stronger? Are you willing to do this? Why or why not?

The family should pursue harmony,
the individual diligence.
Chinese Proverb

# Getting Personal

When a man begins to
understand himself,
he begins to live.
Norvin G. McGranahan

## 92

# Who Do You Love?

Who are the most important people in your life? Do you let these people know how important they are to you? How? Do you make spending time with these people a priority in your life? Why are these people so important to you? Could you ever replace these people if they were gone? Do you spend enough time with these people? If not, how can you change this? Will you change this?

The way to love anything is
to realize that it may be lost.
G. K. Chesterson

## 93

# What Do You Love?

What are your passions in life? What do you love to do? Why do you love these things? Why do you enjoy these things? What do they add to your life? How would you feel if you could no longer enjoy these things? Who do you share these things with? How do you discover what your passions are? Are these things just a passing fancy or are they something that you truly love? How important are these things in your life? Why?

Dost thou love life? Then do not squander time;
for that's the stuff life is made of.
Benjamin Franklin

## 94

# Who are Your Friends?

Who are your true friends? Are they true friends or simply acquaintances? How do you know? Do you know the difference in the two? Do you trust these friends completely? Why or why not? Can they trust you completely? Why or why not? How often do you speak to your friends? How often do you visit your friends or have them visit you? How important are these friends to you? Do you let them know how important they are to you? How? What do they add to your life? What does true friendship mean to you?

If you have one true friend,
you have more than your share comes to.
Thomas Fuller

# 95

## How Do You Live?

Do you live according to the standards that you profess to believe in? Are you true to who you really are? How do you act when no one is around? It is easy to say you believe in this or that, but do you really live what you say you believe? Do you walk the walk or just talk the talk? Are you disciplined in all of the areas of your life? What areas need improvement? What areas are you satisfied with? If you don't live what you say you believe, do you truly believe what you claim to believe?

Take a deep breath of life and
consider how it should be lived.
Don Quixote's Creed

# 96

## Are You Happy?

Are you really happy? Where does happiness come from? Do you depend on other people to make you happy? Are you happy with your career? If not, why not change your career? Are you happy with your life? If not, why not change your life? What do you need to change to be happy? What do you need to do to be happy? Do you really want to be happy or do you enjoy complaining? Are you in the habit of not being a happy person? If so, why? Are you ready to change if you need to?

Happiness depends upon ourselves.
Aristotle

# 97

# How Important is Your Word?

What value do you place on your word? Do you believe that keeping your word is a matter of honor and character? Does that even matter to you? Why or why not? If someone does not keep his or her word, what does that say about that person? When you say something, do you mean it? When you make a promise, do you keep it? Is your word as good as a written contract? Should it be? What do you think? How do you perceive people who don't keep their word? Do you think less of them? Why or why not?

Man by his speech is known to men.
The Havamal

# 98

# How Self-Confident are You?

Are you a confident person? Why or why not? How do you see yourself? Do you have a positive image of yourself or a negative image of yourself? Does your self-confidence change with the situation? If so, what increases your self-confidence? What decreases your self-confidence? What determines how you see yourself? Do you allow other people's opinions to change your view of yourself? How? Why? How important is your self-confidence? What can you do to build more self-confidence? How does your self-confidence or lack thereof, affect your life? Is this acceptable to you? If not, are you willing to change it? Is your self-image dependant solely on your physical appearance? Your financial position or job? How secure are you with who you really are?

What you think about yourself is much
more important than what others think of you.
Seneca

# 99

# Are You Compassionate?

Are you a compassionate person? Do you go out of your way to help others? When? How? Do you speak up for those who need your help? Do you give to charities or to the underprivileged? How do you treat those people who you come in contact with daily? Do you believe that it is better to give than to receive or do you take all that you can get? Do you defend those who can't defend themselves? Is compassion and kindness part of your life? Why or why not? Do you really care about others or is this simply how you prefer to see yourself? If you really care about others, does it show in your actions? Why or why not?

To a person struggling in the sea of life
a few uplifting words may be of great help.
Sai Baba

# 100

## What Are You Thankful For?

Are you thankful for all the blessings in your life? Do you take time to give thanks for what you have or do you waste time worrying about the things that you don't have? Do you count your blessings or do you count your troubles? Do you see the beauty in all things? Do you show gratitude to those who do things for you? Even the small things? Do you think that this is important? Why or why not?

When you arise in the morning, give thanks for the morning light, for your life and strength. Give thanks for your food and the joy of living. If you see no reason for giving thanks, the fault lies in yourself.
Tecumseh

# What Have You Learned?

Make it your business to know
yourself which is the most
difficult lesson in the world.
Cervantes

# 101

# What Secrets has Your
# Soul Revealed to You?

# Afterword

Thank you for your purchase of *Secrets of the Soul*, I hope that you found the questions contained within to be entertaining, as well as enlightening on your journey to self-awareness. If you spent quality time honestly reflecting on each question, you should have a much better idea about who you truly are and what you truly believe after finishing this book. Theodore Parker stated, "The books that help you most are those which make you think the most." It is my fondest hope that *Secrets of the Soul* actually made you think about your beliefs and your philosophy, and provided you with a more profound understanding of who you are.

Hopefully the questions contained in this book have sparked a deep desire in you to ensure that what you truly think is truly what *you* think, and not what someone else wants you to think. Thinking for yourself and knowing what you believe and why you believe what you believe, is the only way to truly be an individual. Let people know the real you – the person who has the courage to think for himself or herself. As Blaise Pascal stated, "The whole dignity of man is in thought. Labor then to think right." Think right, and think for yourself. Only then will you know who you truly are and what you truly believe.

This is only the first step in discovering who you truly are – self-discovery is a life-long adventure. Life is not static; it is ever changing, and so are many of your beliefs. You must constantly rediscover the secret beliefs of your soul as you continue your journey through life. For this reason, it is beneficial for you to keep this book on your bookshelf and refer back to it from time to time to see if the secret beliefs of your soul have changed or remain the same.

It can be interesting to keep a journal of your beliefs as you go through this process and refer back to it to keep track the how your beliefs change over the years. The journey of self-exploration is never-ending and vitally important. As Lao Tzu taught, "Knowing others is wisdom, knowing yourself is enlightenment."

~ Happy Explorations ~

# *Looking for More Wisdom?*

If you are interested in living the warrior lifestyle or simply in living a life of character, integrity and honor you will enjoy The Wisdom Warrior website and newsletter. The Wisdom Warrior website contains dozens of articles, useful links, and news for those seeking to live the warrior lifestyle.

The newsletter is also a valuable resource. Each edition of The Wisdom Warrior Newsletter is packed with motivating quotes, articles, and information which everyone will find useful in their journey to perfect their character and live the life which they were meant to live.

The Wisdom Warrior Newsletter is a newsletter sent directly to your email account and is absolutely FREE! There is no cost or obligation to you whatsoever. You will also receive the current news updates and new articles by Dr. Bohdi Sanders as soon as they are available. Your email address is never shared with anyone else.

All you need to do to start receiving this valuable and informative newsletter is to go to the Wisdom Warrior website and simply sign up. It is that simple! You will find The Wisdom Warrior website at:

## www.TheWisdomWarrior.com

Also, be sure to find posts by Dr. Sanders on Facebook. Dr. Sanders posts enlightening commentaries, photographs, and quotes throughout the week on his Facebook pages. You can find them at:

## www.facebook.com/The.Warrior.Lifestyle

## www.facebook.com/EldersWisdom

## www.facebook.com/bohdi.sanders

Don't miss the opportunity to receive tons of FREE wisdom, enlightening posts, interesting articles, and intriguing photographs on The Wisdom Warrior website and on Dr. Sanders' Facebook pages.

## *Sign Up Today!*

# Other Titles by Bohdi Sanders

Character! Honor! Integrity! Are these traits that guide your life and actions? *Warrior Wisdom: Ageless Wisdom for the Modern Warrior* focuses on how to live your life with character, honor and integrity. This book is highly acclaimed, has won multiple awards and is endorsed by some of the biggest names in martial arts and the world of self-help. *Warrior Wisdom* is filled with wise quotes and useful information for anyone who strives to live a life of excellence. This book will help you live your life to the fullest!

*The Heart and Soul of Bushido* is the second book in the *Warrior Wisdom Series*. Wisdom, life-changing quotes, and entertaining, practical commentaries fill every page. This series has been recognized by four martial arts hall of fame organizations for its inspirational and motivational qualities. The ancient and modern wisdom in this book will definitely help you improve your life and bring meaning to each and every day. The USMAA Hall of Fame awarded Dr. Sanders with Inspiration of the Year for this series!

*The Warrior Lifestyle* is the last installment of the award winning *Warrior Wisdom Series*. Forwarded by martial arts legend Loren W. Christensen, this book has been dubbed as highly inspirational and motivational. If you want to live your life to the fullest, you need to read this one! Don't settle for an ordinary life, make your life extraordinary! The advice and wisdom shines on every page of this book, making it a must read for everyone who strives to live an extraordinary life of character and honor!

# Other Titles by Bohdi Sanders

*Wisdom of the Elders* is a unique, one-of-a-kind quote book. This book is filled with quotes that focus on living life to the fullest with honor, character, and integrity. Honored by the USA Book News with a 1$^{st}$ place award for Best Books of the Year in 2010, this book is a guide for life. *Wisdom of the Elders* contains over 4,800 quotes, all which lead the reader to a life of excellence. If you enjoy quotes, wisdom, and knowledge, you will love this book. This is truly the ultimate quote book for those searching for wisdom!

*The Secrets of Worldly Wisdom* takes the reader deep into the minds of nine of the most revered masters of worldly wisdom. It reveals valuable insights concerning human nature from some of the greatest minds the world has ever known, such as Sun Tzu, Gracian, Goethe, and others. *Worldly Wisdom* presents invaluable lessons for living and advice for avoiding the many pitfalls of human relationships. This is an invaluable and entertaining guidebook for living a successful and rewarding life!

*Modern Bushido* is all about living a life of excellence. This book covers 30 essential traits that will change your life. *Modern Bushido* expands on the standards and principles needed for a life of excellence, and applies them directly to life in today's world. Readers will be motivated and inspired by the straightforward wisdom in this enlightening book. If you want to live a life of excellence, this book is for you! This is a must read for every martial artist and anyone who seeks to live life as it is meant to be lived.

# NOTES

# NOTES

# NOTES

# NOTES

# NOTES